THE SCIENCE OF GOOD VEGAN COOKING

PLANT-BASED EATING, FRUGAL, EASY & DELICIOUS

RACHEL VAUGHAN

VEGAN
RECIPES

22 DAYS
NUTRITION

BREAKFAST
MEALS

22 DAYS
NUTRITION

VANILLA CHIA PUDDING

Makes 2 Servings

INGREDIENTS

6 tablespoons chia seeds
2 cups almond milk
2 tablespoon maple syrup or agave
1 teaspoon vanilla extract
1/2 teaspoon cinnamon

METHOD

1. Blend up the almond milk, vanilla, maple syrup, and cinnamon.

2. Pour liquid mixture over the chia seeds and stir till seeds are evenly mixed in. Stir again five minutes later, and five minutes after that. Let sit for an hour at least, or simply let it sit in the fridge overnight. Serve, topped with fresh fruit of choice.

Pudding will keep in the fridge for up to four days.

QUINOA BREAKFAST PORRIDGE

Serves 2-4

INGREDIENTS

1 cup dry quinoa
2 cups almond milk
1 tbsp agave or maple syrup
1/2 tsp vanilla
1/2 tsp cinnamon
1 tablespoon ground flax meal
Optional toppers and add-ins: sliced banana, fresh berries, a few tablespoons raw walnuts, a tablespoon of chia seeds, a tablespoon of almond butter

METHOD

1. Combine quinoa, almond milk, sweetener, vanilla, and cinnamon in a small pot. Bring to a boil and reduce to a simmer.

2. Allow the quinoa to cook until all of the liquid is absorbed and quinoa is fluffy (15-20 minutes). Stir in the flax meal. Stir in any additional toppers or add-ins, and enjoy.

Leftovers will keep in the fridge for up to three days and can be reheated with almond milk over the stove.

BANANA AND ALMOND BUTTER OATS

Serves 2

INGREDIENTS

1 cup gluten free rolled oats
1 cup almond milk

1 cup water
1 teaspoon cinnamon
2 tablespoons almond butter
1 banana, sliced

METHOD

1. Bring the water and almond milk to a boil in a small pot. Add the oats and reduce to a simmer.

2. Cook until oats have absorbed all liquid. Stir in cinnamon. Top with almond butter and banana, and serve.

GLUTEN FREE, VEGAN BANANA PANCAKES

Serves 2-3

INGREDIENTS

1 cup all purpose, gluten free flour
1 1/2 tsp baking powder
1/2 tsp cinnamon
Dash sea salt
1 tsp apple cider vinegar
2/3 cup almond milk
1 ripe banana
1 teaspoon vanilla
1 tbsp + 2 tsp melted coconut oil, divided

METHOD

1. Mix the flour, baking powder, cinnamon, and sea salt together.

2. Add the vinegar to the almond milk and whisk together till froth. Add the almond/vinegar mixture to a blender, along with the banana, vanilla, and 1 tbsp coconut oil. Blend till smooth.

3. Mix the liquid mixture into the flour mixture till just combined.

4. Heat 2 tsp coconut oil in a nonstick skillet. Add the batter, heaping 1/4 cup at a time. Let the pancakes cook till bubbles form on the top; then flip and continue cooking till pancakes are cooked through. Repeat with all remaining batter.

5. Serve pancakes with fresh berries.

APPLE CINNAMON OATMEAL

Serves 2

INGREDIENTS

1 cup gluten free rolled oats
1 cup water
3/4 cup almond milk
3/4 cup diced apples
1/2 teaspoon cinnamon or pumpkin pie spice
2 tbsp maple syrup
1/4 cup chopped raw walnut pieces

METHOD

1. Combine the oats, water, almond milk, apples, cinnamon and syrup in a medium pot or saucepan. Bring to a boil and lower to a simmer. Cook until oats have absorbed the liquid and apples are tender (about 10-15 minutes).

2. Divide oats into two bowls and top with raw walnut pieces. Enjoy.

STRAWBERRY GINGER CHIA PUDDING

Makes 2 servings

INGREDIENTS

6 tbsp chia seeds
1 cup frozen or regular strawberries
1 3/4 cups almond milk
3/4 tsp ginger powder (substitute cinnamon if you prefer)
1 tablespoon maple syrup

METHOD

1. Blend the strawberries, milk, ginger, and sweetener together on high till smooth.

2. Pour liquid over the chia seeds, and stir every couple of minutes for the next fifteen minutes. Let sit for a few hours or overnight in the fridge. Serve.

BANANA BREAKFAST WRAPS

Serves 2

INGREDIENTS

2 large bananas
4 Boston or butter lettuce leaves
4 tbsp almond butter
4 tsp maple syrup

METHOD

1. Spread each lettuce leaf with a tablespoon of almond butter.

2. Cut the bananas in half. Place half of a banana in each leaf. Drizzle each with a teaspoon of maple syrup and serve.

GLUTEN FREE, VEGAN PUMPKIN MUFFINS

Makes 12 muffins

INGREDIENTS

2 cups gluten free, all purpose flour
2 tsp baking powder
1 tsp baking soda
2 tsp pumpkin pie spice

1/2 tsp. salt
1 teaspoon apple cider vinegar
1 cup almond milk
2 tbsp melted coconut oil
1/2 cup cup maple syrup
3/4 cup pumpkin puree
1/2 cup raisins (optional)

METHOD

1. Pre-heat oven to 350 degrees lightly grease a muffin tin.

2. Mix together the flour, baking powder, baking soda, pumpkin pie spice, and salt in a large mixing bowl.

3. In a separate mixing bowl, whisk together the apple cider vinegar and almond milk till frothy. Mix in the oil, syrup, and pumpkin puree.

4. Pour the wet ingredients into the dry ingredients and mix till they're just combined—don't overmix. Fold in the raisins.

5. Spoon the batter into muffin tins and bake for about 20- 25 minutes, or until a toothpick inserted into the center of a muffin comes out clean.

Muffins will keep for up to three days in an airtight container, or can be frozen.

12

LUNCH
MEALS

Serves 2

INGREDIENTS

For the salad:

3 cups thinly shredded red cabbage
I large granny smith apple, shredded
2 tbsp hemp seeds

For the dressing:

1/4 cup tahini
3 tablespoons water
2 teaspoons agave nectar or maple syrup
1/2 teaspoon sesame oil
1/4 – 1/2 tsp sea salt (to taste)
I tablespoon apple cider vinegar

METHOD

1. Whisk dressing ingredients together and set aside.

2. Dress the shredded vegetables and hemp seeds with dressing; you can use as much as you like, but make sure you coat everything well (a half cup will probably suffice). Serve.

Slaw will keep in the fridge overnight.

GOLDEN HARVEST KALE SALAD

Serves 2

INGREDIENTS

For the salad:

5 cups washed, dried, and chopped kale (about I bunch after preparation)
2 small carrots, grated
2 stalk celery, chopped
4 tbsp golden raisins
4 tbsp chopped walnuts
I apple, sliced thin

For the dressing:

2 tbsp olive oil
I 1/2 tbsp apple cider
I tbsp agave
Salt and pepper to taste

METHOD

1. Whisk the dressing ingredients together, and set aside.

2. In a big mixing bowl, pour about the dressing onto the chopped kale, and begin "massaging" it with your hands, until the kale starts to get soft and well coated. It should develop even a wilted texture.

2. Add the remaining salad ingredients, and toss the whole salad again.

3. Plate the salad, and top it with your sliced apple. Enjoy. Leftovers will keep overnight in the fridge.

SMOKY AVOCADO AND JICAMA SALAD

Serves 2

INGREDIENTS

For the dressing:

1 small avocado
1 tbsp cumin powder
Juice of 2 limes
1/2 teaspoon smoked paprika
1 cup water
1/4 tsp salt
Dash cayenne pepper

For the salad:

1 heaping cup shredded cabbage
1 heaping cup shredded carrot
10 large leaves romaine lettuce, sliced thinly
2 cups jicama, cut into matchsticks
2 tbsp toasted pumpkin seeds

METHOD

1. Blend all dressing ingredients together in a blender or processor till smooth.

2. Pour dressing over this salad, and toss. Serve.

MANGO, KALE, AND AVOCADO SALAD

Serves 2

INGREDIENTS:

1 bunch curly kale, de-stemmed, chopped, washed, and dried (about 6 cups after preparation)
Juice of 1 large lemon
2 teaspoons flax or olive oil
1 teaspoon sesame oil
2 teaspoons maple syrup or agave nectar
Sea salt to taste
1 chopped red bell pepper

1 cup mango, cut into small cubes
1 small Haas avocado, cut into cubes

METHOD

1. "Massage" the lemon juice, flax/olive and sesame oils, syrup, and salt into the kale till it's wilted and dressed evenly.

2. Mix in the pepper, mango, and avocado cubes. Toss well to combine. Serve.

ROASTED BUTTERNUT SQUASH AND APPLE SOUP

Makes 4 servings

INGREDIENTS

1 butternut squash, peeled and chopped (about 3-4 lbs, or 4-5 cups)
3 small apples, roughly chopped
1 very small onion, chopped
2 tbsp melted coconut oil
1/2 tsp kosher or sea salt (+more to taste)
Black pepper to taste
1/4 tsp nutmeg
1/2 tsp crushed thyme
2 1/2 cups low sodium vegetable broth
1/2 cup canned coconut milk

METHOD

1. Place squash, apples, and onion on a large roasting tray. Drizzle coconut oil and salt and pepper over them, mix with your hands, and roast at 375 degrees for about 45 minutes, or until they're all soft and golden.

2. Place roasted veggies in a blender with vegetable broth, nutmeg, coconut milk, and thyme. Blend, and season to taste with salt and pepper. If the soup needs more liquid, add some more, until it reaches the consistency you like.

3. Transfer soup to a pot, re-heat and serve.

EASY CURRIED YELLOW LENTILS WITH AVOCADO "CROUTONS"

Serves 4

INGREDIENTS

3/4 cup onion, diced
1 1/2 tbsp coconut oil
1 cup yellow lentils
1 sweet potato, cut into 1 1/2 inch cubes
2 carrots, diced (optional, but I had them, so I used them!)
1/2 tsp turmeric
1 tbsp mild curry powder
1 tsp powdered ginger
1/2 tsp sea salt
Black pepper to taste
4 cups vegetable broth or water

METHOD

1. Heat oil in a large pot over medium heat. Saute onion till its turning translucent and a little golden. Add the lentils, potato, carrots, and spices/seasonings, and stir to combine everything.

2. Add the broth or water to the pot and bring to a boil. Reduce to a simmer and cook for 25 minutes, or until the lentils and sweet potato are tender.

3. Allow lentils to cool a bit, then serve with fresh avocado slices.

KALE SALAD WITH CARROTS, APPLES, RAISINS, AND CREAMY CURRY DRESSING

Serves 2-4

INGREDIENTS

For the dressing:

1/2 cup raw cashews or walnuts
2 tablespoons lemon juice
2 pitted dates
1/2 cup water
1/2 tsp sea salt
2 tsp curry powder

For the salad:

1 head kale, de-stemmed, washed, dried, and cut into bite sized pieces (about 5 cups)
2 large carrots, peeled and chopped
1 large apple, chopped into small pieces
1/3 cup raisins
1/2 cup chickpeas

METHOD

1. Blend all dressing ingredients in a high speed blender till smooth.

2. Massage the kale with the dressing, making sure that everything is well coated and softened (start with 1/2 cup dressing and add as needed—you may have some leftover). Add the apple, carrot, raisins, and chickpeas, and remix the salad, adding more dressing if you like. Serve.

RED QUINOA, ALMOND AND ARUGULA SALAD WITH CANTELOUPE

Makes 2 servings

INGREDIENTS

1 1/2 cups fresh cantaloupe, cut into 1 inch chunks
1 1/2 cups red quinoa (regular quinoa is also totally fine)
4 cups arugula, tightly packed
1/4 cup slivered, crumbled, or sliced almonds
2 tablespoons flax, hemp, or olive oil
1 tablespoon apple cider vinegar
1 teaspoon maple syrup

Sea salt and black pepper to taste

METHOD

1. Whisk together the oil, vinegar, syrup, and seasoning.

2. Divide the arugula, quinoa, and melon onto two serving plates. Sprinkle them with almonds and then drizzle the dressing over them.

SPICY THAI SALAD

Serves 2

INGREDIENTS

For the dressing:

1 avocado
1 cup coconut water
¼ cup cilantro
¼ cup basil
¼ tsp salt (or more)
2 pitted dates
1 tbsp minced or grated ginger
Sprinkle of cayenne pepper

For the salad:

1 bell pepper, chopped
2 cups grated carrots
1/2 cup cilantro, chopped
1 cup sprouts
2 cups shredded romaine lettuce
1 cup sliced cucumbers

METHOD

1. Blend all dressing ingredients in a high speed blender till smooth.

2. Top salad with dressing as desired. Serve.

CARROT AVOCADO BISQUE

Serves 2

INGREDIENTS

2 cups carrot juice
1/2 Haas avocado
1 tablespoon low sodium tamari
1 teaspoon grated ginger

METHOD

Blend all ingredients in a high speed blender till smooth.

GLUTEN FREE TORTILLA PIZZA

Serves 2

INGREDIENTS

2 10" brown rice tortillas (Food for Life brand)
2/3 cup low sodium, organic marinara sauce, divided
2 cups vegetable + toppings of choice (broccoli, spinach, peppers, mushrooms, olives, artichokes, roasted potato, etc)
1/2 cup basic cashew cheese (recipe below)

METHOD

1. Preheat oven to 400 F. Place tortillas on a foil or parchment lined baking sheet. Bake for 5-8 minutes, or until slightly crispy.

2. Remove tortillas from oven. Top with tomato sauce and veggies, and return to oven for 8-10 more minutes (till toppings are cooked through). Dot with cashew cheese, and serve.

NB: If you don't have cashew cheese, you can simply sprinkle pizzas with nutritional yeast. You can also use red pepper hummus in place of the tomato sauce.

BASIC CASHEW CHEESE

Makes 1 cup

INGREDIENTS

1 1/4 cups cashews, soaked for at least three hours (or overnight) and drained
1/2 tsp sea salt
1 small clove garlic, minced (optional)
2 tbsp lemon juice
1/3-1/2 cup water
1/4 cup nutritional yeast

METHOD

Place the cashews, sea salt, garlic, lemon, and 1/3 cup water in a food processor. Process till the mixture is very smooth and soft (you're aiming for a texture similar to creamy ricotta cheese), stopping to scrape the bowl down a few times and adding a little extra water as necessary.

ROASTED CAULIFLOWER AND PARSNIP SOUP

Yields 4 servings

INGREDIENTS

1 medium head cauliflower, chopped
4 large parsnips, peeled and chopped
1-2 tbsp olive oil
4 shallots, cut in half
1 clove garlic, minced

1 tsp thyme
1/2 tsp sage
4 cups vegetable broth
1/2 cup almond or coconut milk
Sea salt and pepper to taste
Paprika

METHOD

1. Preheat oven to 400 degrees. Line a baking tray or two with tin foil.

2. Lay cauliflower, parsnips, shallots, and garlic, out on foil, and drizzle with olive oil, thyme, sage, salt and pepper.

3. Roast veggies for about 35-40 min, or until they're soft and golden brown.

4. Place veggies in a high speed blender (you may have to work in batches) and add broth and non-dairy milk. Blend until soup is smooth and creamy, adding more liquid if you need to. Alternately, you can use an immersion blender.

5. Transfer soup to a pot and re-season to taste with salt and pepper.

SNACKS

HEMP HUMMUS

Serves 4

INGREDIENTS

1/4 cup shelled hemp seeds
1 can chickpeas, drained, or 2 cups freshly cooked chickpeas
1/2 tsp salt (to taste)
2-3 tbsp freshly squeezed lemon juice (to taste)
1 small clove garlic, minced
1 tbsp tahini (optional)
1/2 tsp cumin
Water as needed

METHOD

1. Place the hemp seeds in the bowl of a food processor and grind till powdery.

2. Add the chickpeas, salt, lemon, garlic, tahini, and cumin, and begin to process. Add water in a thin stream (stopping to scrape the bowl a few times) until the mixture is totally smooth and creamy.

3. Garnish with extra hemp seeds and serve.

Hummus will keep in the fridge for up to four days.

RAW PEANUT BUTTER AND JELLY SNACK BALLS

Makes 20 Balls

INGREDIENTS

1 1/2 cups organic roasted, unsalted peanuts
1 1/2 cups dark raisins
2 tablespoons peanut butter
Pinch sea salt

METHOD

1. Add all ingredients to a food processor and process till the peanuts are broken down and the mixture is starting to stick together. It may release a little oil, but that's OK.

2. Roll mixture into 1 inch balls. Store in the fridge for at least thirty minutes before serving.

SWEET POTATO HUMMUS

Serves 6

INGREDIENTS

2 cups sweet potato, steamed or baked and cut into cubes
1 can organic, low sodium chickpeas, drained (or 1 1/2 cups cooked chickpeas)
1 1/2 tsp sesame oil
1/4 cup tahini
1 tablespoon lemon juice
1/2 tsp smoked paprika
1/2 tsp salt
Black pepper to taste
1/2 cup water + more as needed

METHOD

1. Place sweet potato, chickpeas, sesame oil, tahini, lemon, salt and pepper into a food processor. Pulse to combine.

2. Turn on the motor and drizzle in 1/2 water. Process mixture, stopping a few times to scrape down the bowl. Add more water as needed until you have a creamy, smooth textured hummus. Serve.

DRESSINGS

TURMERIC TAHINI DRESSING

Makes 1 1/2 Cups

INGREDIENTS

1/2 cup tahini
2 tablespoons apple cider vinegar
2 tablespoons coconut aminos or tamari
1/2 teaspoon ground ginger (or 1 teaspoon fresh, grated ginger)
2 teaspoons turmeric
1 teaspoon maple syrup
2/3 - 3/4 cup water

METHOD

Blend all ingredients together in a blender or food processor till smooth. Start with 2/3 cup water and add more as needed (dressing will thicken in the fridge).

WALNUT PESTO

Makes 1 generous cup

INGREDIENTS

1 cup coarsely chopped walnuts
2 1/2 cups packed fresh basil leaves, rinsed and dried
1 large garlic clove
1 tbsp lemon zest
Juice of 1 lemon
1/4 cup nutritional yeast
1/2 cup good extra virgin olive oil
Salt and pepper to taste

METHOD

1. Grind walnuts in a food processor till finely ground. Add basil and pulse till it forms a coarse mixture.

2. Add the garlic, lemon zest and juice, and nutritional yeast, and pulse a few more times. Turn motor on and run as you add olive oil in a thin stream. I like my pesto very thick, but add more oil if you like a thinner mix. Add salt and pepper to taste. Use, or freeze as needed.

BALSAMIC TAHINI DRESSING

Makes 1 1/4 cups

INGREDIENTS

1/2 cup tahini
1/4 cup balsamic vinegar
1/2 cup water
1/4 tsp garlic powder, or 1/2 clove finely minced garlic
1 tbsp tamari or nama shoyu

METHOD

Blend all ingredients together in a blender or food processor. Add more water as needed.

RAW RANCH DRESSING

Makes 1 ½ cups

INGREDIENTS

¾ cup cashews, soaked for at least two hours and drained
½ cup water
2 tbsp lemon juice
¼ cup apple cider vinegar
¼-½ tsp salt
½ tsp dried thyme
½ tsp dried oregano

1 clove garlic
3 tbsp fresh dill
3 tbsp fresh parsley
3 tbsp olive oil

METHOD

Blend all ingredients in a high speed blender and serve.

CREAMY APRICOT GINGER DRESSING

Makes nearly 2 cups (recipe can be halved)

INGREDIENTS

1/2 cup dried apricots, packed
3/4 inch long knob raw ginger (or 1/2 tsp ginger powder)
1/2 cup orange juice
1/2 cup water
2 tbsp apple cider vinegar
1 tbsp tamari or nama shoyu
2 tbsp olive oil

METHOD

Blend all dressing ingredients together in a high speed blender and serve.

Fig and White Balsamic Vinaigrette

Makes 1 1/4 cups

INGREDIENTS

6 very large dried figs (if yours are small, add a few more), soaked for about 8 hours and drained
1/3 white balsamic vinegar (sub regular if need be)
1/4 cup olive oil
1/4 water
1 small clove garlic
1 tbsp dijon mustard
Salt and black pepper to taste

METHOD

Blend all ingredients in a high speed blender till totally smooth and creamy. Add more water if it's too thick.

DINNER
MEALS

22DAYS
NUTRITION

Serves 4

INGREDIENTS

For the salad:

1 cup dry quinoa, rinsed
Dash salt
2 cups vegetable broth or water
1/2 large cucumber, diced neatly
1 small bell pepper, diced neatly
1 can BPA free, organic black beans
10-15 basil leaves, chopped into a chiffonade
1/4 cup fresh cilantro, chopped

For the vinaigrette:

2 tbsp extra virgin olive oil
1/4 cup apple cider vinegar
1 tbsp agave or maple syrup
1 tbsp dijon mustard
1 tsp cumin
Salt and pepper to taste

METHOD

1. Rinse quinoa through a sieve till the water runs clear. Transfer it to a small or medium sized pot and add two cups of vegetable broth or water and dash of salt. Bring to a boil, then reduce to a simmer. Cover the pot so that the lid is on, but there's a small gap where water can escape. Simmer till quinoa has absorbed all of the liquid and is fluffy (about 15-20 minutes).

2. Transfer cooked quinoa to a mixing bowl. Add chopped vegetables, black beans, and herbs.

3. Whisk dressing ingredients. Add the dressing to the salad, and serve. (If you don't feel that you need all the dressing, just add as much as you'd like to.)

Salad will keep for three days in the fridge.

ZUCCHINI PASTA WITH CHERRY TOMATOES, BASIL, SWEET POTATO, AND HEMP PARMESAN

Serves 2

INGREDIENTS

2 large zucchini
1 red bell pepper, diced
15 cherry tomatoes, quartered
8 large basil leaves, chiffonaded
2 small sweet potato, baked and then cut into cubes
2 tbsp balsamic vinegar
1 small avocado, cubed

4 tbsp hemp parmesan (recipe below)

METHOD

1. Use a spiralizer or a julienne peeler to cut zucchini into long ribbons (resembling noodles).

2. Toss zucchini with all remaining ingredients, and serve.

Hemp Parmesan

Makes 1/2 - 2/3 cup

INGREDIENTS

6 tbsp hemp seeds
6 tbsp nutritional yeast
Dash sea salt

METHOD

Combine all ingredients in a food processor, and pulse to break down and combine. Store in the fridge for up to 2 weeks.

GLUTEN FREE WHITE BEAN AND SUMMER VEGETABLE PASTA

Serves 4

INGREDIENTS

1 small eggplant, cut into 1 inch cubes and lightly salted for 30 minutes, then patted dry
1 clove garlic, minced
1 large zucchini, sliced
1 can organic fire roasted, diced tomatoes
1 small can organic tomato sauce
1 tsp agave
1 tbsp dried basil
1 tsp dried oregano
1 tsp dried thyme
1 can (or 2 cups freshly cooked) cannellini or navy beans, drained
8 oz. dry brown rice or quinoa pasta (rigatoni, linguine, and penne are all fine)

METHOD

1. Heat a large skillet with olive or coconut oil spray (or just use a few tbsp water). Sautee the eggplant with the garlic till the eggplant is getting nice and brown (about 8 minutes).

2. Add the zucchini and cook it till tender (another 5 minutes).

3. Add the canned tomatoes, tomato sauce, agave, basil, oregano, thyme. Heat through. Test for seasoning, and add more of whatever herbs you like.

4. Add the white beans and heat the whole sauce through. This is so tasty and simple, you could eat it on its own as a "cheater's" ratatouille.

5. While your sauce cooks, put a pot of salted water to boil. Add pasta when it hits a rolling boil, and cook pasta till tender

but still a little al dente.

6. Drain pasta, smother with sauce, and serve.

Leftovers will keep for three days in the fridge.

BUTTERNUT SQUASH CURRY

Serves 4

INGREDIENTS

1 tablespoon melted coconut oil
1 white or yellow onion, chopped
1 clove garlic, minced
1 tablespoon fresh ginger, minced
3 tablespoons red curry paste
1 tablespoon organic sugar or coconut sugar
2/3 cups vegetable broth
One 14- or 15-ounce can coconut milk
1 tablespoon soy sauce or tamari
1 green or red bell pepper, chopped
1 pound butternut squash
2 cups green beans, cut into 2" pieces
1 to 2 tablespoon lime juice

METHOD

1. Heat the coconut oil in a large pot or wok. Add the onion and cook till it's soft and translucent (5 to 8 minutes).

2. Add the garlic and ginger and let them cook for about a minute. Then, add the curry paste and sugar. Mix the ingredients together until the paste is evenly incorporated.

3. Whisk in the broth, the coconut milk, and the tamari. Add the red pepper and butternut squash. Simmer till the squash is totally tender (25 to 30 minutes minutes). If you need to add extra broth as the mixture cooks, do so.

4. Stir in the green beans and let them cook for two or three minutes, or until tender. Season the curry to taste with extra soy sauce or tamari and stir in the lime juice as desired. Remove from heat and serve over quinoa or brown basmati rice.

Leftovers will keep for four days.

RAW ZUCCHINI ALFREDO WITH BASIL AND CHERRY TOMATOES

Serves 2 (with leftover alfredo sauce)

INGREDIENTS

Pasta

2 large zucchini
1 cup cherry tomatoes, halved
1/4 cup basil, sliced

Raw alfredo sauce

1 cup cashews, soaked for at least three hours (or overnight) and drained
1/3 cup water
1 tsp agave or maple syrup
1 clove garlic
3-4 tbsp lemon juice (to taste)
1/4 cup nutritional yeast
1/4 tsp sea salt

1. Use a spiralizer or a julienne peeler to cut zucchini into long ribbons (resembling noodles).

2. Add tomatoes and basil to the zucchini noodles and set them all aside in a large mixing bowl.

3. Blend all of the alfredo sauce ingredients together in a high speed blender till smooth.

4. Cover the pasta in 1/2 cup sauce, and mix it in well, adding additional sauce as needed (you'll have some sauce left-over). Serve.

BLACK BEAN AND CORN BURGERS

Makes 4 Burgers

INGREDIENTS

1 tablespoon coconut oil
1 small yellow onion, chopped
1 cup fresh, frozen or canned organic corn kernels
1 can organic, low sodium black beans, drained (or 1 1/2 cups cooked black beans)
1 cup brown rice, cooked
1/4 cup oat flour (or ground, rolled oats)
1/4 cup tomato paste
2 tsp cumin
1 heaping tsp paprika
1 heaping tsp chili powder
1/2 - 1 tsp sea salt (to taste)
Black pepper or red pepper, to taste

METHOD

1. Preheat your oven to 350 F.

2. Heat the coconut oil in a large sauté pan. Add the onion and saute till onion is golden, soft, and fragrant (about 5-8 minutes).

2) Add corn, beans and tomato paste to the pan and heat through.

3) Place cooked rice into the bowl of a food processor. Add the beans, onion, tomato paste, and corn mixture. Pulse to combine. Add spices, oat flour, and a touch of water, if you need it. Pulse more, until you have a thick and sticky (but pliable) mixture. If the mixture is too wet, add a tablespoon or two of additional oat flour.

4) Shape into 4 burgers and place burgers on a foil lined baking sheet. Bake for 25 -30 minutes, or until burgers are lightly crisped, flipping once through. Serve with fresh guacamole, if desired!

Serves 4

INGREDIENTS

For rollatini:

2 large eggplant, sliced lengthwise into 1/4 inch thick slices
Olive oil
1 1/4 cups cashews, soaked for at least three hours (or overnight) and drained
1/2 tsp sea salt
1 small clove garlic, minced (optional)
2 tbsp lemon juice
1/3-1/2 cup water
1/4 cup nutritional yeast
2 tsps dried basil
1 tsp dried oregano
Black pepper to taste
1/2 10 oz. package frozen spinach, defrosted and squeezed thoroughly to remove all excess liquid (I press mine firmly through a sieve)
1 1/2 cups organic, low sodium marinara sauce

METHOD

1. Preheat oven to 400 F. Slice eggplants lengthwise into strips about 1/2" thick. Place eggplant slices onto baking sheets and sprinkle well with sea salt or kosher salt. Let sit for 30 minutes; this decreases bitterness and removes excess moisture. Pat the slices dry, and spray them or brush them lightly with olive oil.

2. Roast eggplant slices till browning (about 20 min), flipping halfway through.

3. While eggplant is roasting, make the cashew cheese. Place the cashews, sea salt, garlic, lemon, and 1/3 cup water in a food processor. Process till the mixture is very smooth and soft (you're aiming for a texture similar to creamy ricotta cheese), stopping to scrape the bowl down a few times and adding a little extra water as necessary. Stop the motor, and add the nutritional yeast, basil, oregano, and black pepper. Process again to incorporate. Transfer the cashew cheese to a bowl and mix in the chopped spinach. Set the cheese mixture aside.

4. Remove the roasted eggplant from the oven and reduce heat to 325 F. Allow the slices to cool until they can be handled. Transfer them to a cutting board and add about 3 tbsp of the cheese mixture to the end of one side. Roll up from that side, and place seam down in a small casserole dish. Repeat with all remaining slices.

5. Smother the eggplant rolls with tomato sauce, and bake, uncovered, for about 20-25 minutes, or until hot. Serve with sides of choice.

GINGER LIME CHICKPEA SWEET POTATO BURGERS

Makes 4-6 Burgers

INGREDIENTS

3/4 cup cooked chickpeas
1/2 small onion
1 inch ginger, chopped
1 tsp coconut oil

1 1/2 cups sweet potato, baked or steamed and cubed
1/3 cup quinoa flakes or gluten free rolled oats
2 heaping tbsp flax meal
2-3 tbsp lime juice (to taste)
2 tbsp low sodium tamari
1/4 cup cilantro, chopped
Dash red pepper flakes (optional)
Water as needed

METHOD

1. Preheat oven to 350 F.

2. Heat coconut oil in a large pan or wok. Saute onion and ginger in 1 tsp coconut oil (or coconut oil spray) till soft and fragrant (about 5 minutes). Add chickpeas and heat through.

3. Place the chickpeas, onion, and ginger in a food processor and add the sweet potato, quinoa flakes or oats, flax seed, lime juice, cilantro, tamari or coconut aminos, and dash of red pepper flakes, if using. Pulse to combine, then run the motor and add some water until consistency is very thick but easy to mold.

4. Shape mixture into 4-6 burgers. Bake at 350 degrees for about 35 minutes, flipping halfway through.

SWEET POTATO AND BLACK BEAN CHILI

Serves 6

INGREDIENTS

1 1/2 cup dried black beans
4 cups sweet potato, diced into 3/4 inch cubes
1 tablespoon olive oil
1 1/2 cups chopped white or yellow onion
2 cloves garlic, minced
1 chipotle pepper en adobo, chopped finely
2 teaspoons cumin powder
1/2 teaspoon smoked paprika
1 tablespoon ground chili powder
1 14 or 15 ounce can of organic, diced tomatoes (I like the Muir Glen brand)
1 can organic, low sodium black beans (or 1 1/2 cups cooked black beans)
2 cups low sodium vegetable broth
Sea salt to taste

METHOD

1. Heat the tablespoon of oil in a dutch oven or a large pot. Saute the onion for a few minutes, then add the sweet potato and garlic. Keep sauteing until the onions are soft, about 8-10 minutes.

2. Add the chili en adobo, the cumin, the chili powder, and the smoked paprika. Heat until the spices are very fragrant. Add the tomatoes, black beans, and vegetable broth.

3. When broth is bubbling, reduce to a simmer and cook for approximately 25-30 minutes, or until the sweet potatoes are tender.

4. Add more broth as needed, and season to taste with salt. Serve.

Leftover chili can be frozen and will keep for up to five days.

RAW CAULIFLOWER RICE WITH LEMON, MINT, AND PISTACHIOS

Serves 2

INGREDIENTS

5 cups raw cauliflower florets
I oz pistachios
1/4 cup each basil and mint
2 tsp lemon zest
I 1/2 tbsp lemon juice
I tbsp olive oil
1/4 cup dried currants
Sea salt and black pepper to taste

METHOD

1. Transfer 3 cups of the cauliflower to a food processor. Process until the cauliflower is broken down into pieces that are about the size of rice. Transfer to a large mixing bowl.

2. Transfer remaining 2 cups of cauliflower to the food processor. Add the pistachios. Process, once again, until cauliflower is broken down into rice sized pieces. Pulse in the basil and mint till herbs are finely chopped.

3. Add the additional chopped cauliflower, pistachios, and herbs to the mixing bowl with the first batch of cauliflower. Add the lemon juice, oil, and currents. Season to taste with salt and pepper. Serve.

BROWN RICE AND LENTIL SALAD

Serves 4

INGREDIENTS

2 tablespoons olive oil
I tablespoon apple cider vinegar
I tablespoon lemon juice
I tablespoon dijon mustard
1/2 tsp smoked paprika
Sea salt and black pepper to taste
2 cups cooked brown rice
I 15-oz can organic, no sodium added lentils, rinsed, or 1 1/ cups cooked lentils
I carrot, diced or grated
4 tbsp chopped fresh parsley

METHOD

1. Whisk oil, vinegar, lemon juice, mustard, paprika, salt and pepper together in a large bowl.

2. Add the rice, lentils, carrot and parsley. Mix well and serve.

RAW "PEANUT" NOODLES

Serves 2

INGREDIENTS

For the dressing:

I tablespoon grated ginger
1/2 cup olive oil
2 tsp sesame oil (toasted)
2 tbsp mellow white miso
3 dates, pitted, or ¼ cup maple syrup
I tbsp nama shoyu
1/4 cup water

For the noodles:

2 zucchinis
I red bell pepper, sliced into matchsticks
I carrot, grated
I small cucumber, peeled into thin strips
I cup thinly sliced, steamed snow peas
1/4 cup chopped scallions or green onion

METHOD

1. Blend dressing ingredients in a high speed blender until all ingredients are creamy and smooth.

2. Use a spiralizer or julienne peeler to cut the zucchini into long, thin "noodles." Combine the zucchini with the pepper, carrot, cucumber, and scallions.

3. Dress the noodles with enough dressing to coat them well. Serve.

EASY FRIED RICE AND VEGETABLES

Serves 2

INGREDIENTS

2 tsp toasted sesame oil
I tbsp grated ginger
I 1/2 cups cooked brown rice
2-3 cups frozen or fresh vegetables of choice
I tbsp low sodium tamari
I tbsp rice vinegar
Vegetable broth as needed

METHOD

1. Heat the sesame oil in a large wok. Add the grated ginger and heat it for a minute or two.

2. Add the brown rice and vegetables. Saute till the vegetables are tender.

3. Add the tamari, rice vinegar, and a splash of vegetable broth if the mixture is dry. Serve.

Serves 2

INGREDIENTS

For the salad:

4 heaping cups arugula (or other green)
I lb butternut squash, peeled and chopped
I small head cauliflower, washed and chopped into small florets
2 tbsp coconut or olive oil
Sea salt and pepper to taste
1/4 cup raw pumpkin seeds
1/4 cup goji berries

For the dressing:

3 tbsp olive oil
2 tbsp orange juice
I tbsp lemon juice
1/2 tsp turmeric
1/4 tsp ground ginger
I tbsp agave or maple syrup
Sea salt to taste

METHOD

1. Toss the squash in I tbsp oil and season with salt and pepper. Toss the cauliflower in the other tablespoon and season with salt and pepper. Roast both veggies at 375 degrees for 20-30 minutes (the cauliflower will cook faster), till golden brown and fragrant. Remove from oven and let cool.

2. Place the arugula, goji berries, and pumpkin seeds in a large bowl. Add roasted vegetables. Whisk together the olive oil, lemon juice, turmeric, maple syrup or agave, ginger, and sea salt, and dress all the veggies.

3. Divide salad onto two plates, and serve.

ROASTED VEGETABLE PESTO PASTA SALAD

Note: Instead of using brown rice or quinoa pasta in this dish, you can also mix the roasted vegetables and pesto into a whole grain, like brown rice or millet or quinoa, for a more wholesome variation.

Serves 4

INGREDIENTS

3 cups zucchini, chopped into 3/4" pieces
3 cups eggplant, chopped into 3/4" pieces
I large Jersey or heirloom tomato, chopped
2 tbsp olive oil or melted coconut oil
Sea salt and black pepper to taste
8 oz brown rice or quinoa pasta (penne and fusilli work well)
1/2 - 2/3 cup walnut pesto (see: dressings)

METHOD

1. Preheat your oven to 400 F.

2. Lay the zucchini, eggplant and tomato out on two parchment or foil lined baking sheets and drizzle with the olive or coconut oil. Coat the vegetables with the oil and roast vegetables for thirty minutes, or until tender and browning.

3. While vegetables roast, bring a pot of salted water to boil. Add the pasta and cook till al dente (according to package instructions). Drain pasta and set aside in a large mixing bowl.

4. Add the roasted vegetables and to the pasta. Mix in the pesto, season to taste, and serve at once.

PORTOBELLO "STEAK" AND CAULIFLOWER "MASHED POTATOES"

Serves 4

INGREDIENTS

For the mushrooms:

1/4 cup olive oil
3 tbsp balsamic vinegar
3 tbsp low sodium tamari or nama shoyu
3 tbsp maple syrup
Sprinkle pepper
4 portobello mushroom caps, cleaned

Submerge 4 Portobello caps in the marinade. 1 hour will be enough for them to be ready, but overnight in the fridge is even better.

For the Cauliflower Mashed Potatoes:

1 cups cashews, raw
4 cups cauliflower, chopped into small florets and pieces
2 tbsp mellow white miso
3 tbsp nutritional yeast
2 tbsp lemon juice
Sea salt and black pepper to taste
1/3 cup (or less) water

METHOD

1. Place cashews into the bowl of your food processor, and process into a fine powder.

2. Add the miso, lemon juice, nutritional yeast, pepper and cauliflower. Pulse to combine. With the motor of the machine running, add water in a thin stream, until the mixture begins to take on a smooth, whipped texture. You may need to stop frequently to clean the sides of the bowl and help it along.

3. When the mix resembles mashed potatoes, stop, scoop, and serve alongside a Portobello cap.

QUINOA ENCHILADAS

Adapted from a recipe in Food52

Serves 6

INGREDIENTS

1 tbsp coconut oil
2 cloves garlic, minced
1 small yellow onion, chopped
3/4 pounds baby bella mushrooms, chopped
1/2 cup diced green chilis
1/2 teaspoon ground cumin
1/4 teaspoon sea salt (or to taste)
1 can organic, low sodium black beans or 1 1/2 cup cooked black beans
1 1/2 cup cooked quinoa
10 6-inch corn tortillas
1 1/4 cup organic, low sodium tomato or enchilada sauce

METHOD

1. Preheat oven to 350 degrees.

2. In a large pot over medium heat, heat coconut oil. Sautee onion and garlic till onion is translucent (about 5-8 min). Add mushrooms and cook until liquid has been released and evaporated (another 5 min).

3. Add the chilis to the pot and give them a stir for 2 minutes. Add the cumin, sea salt, black beans and quinoa, and continue heating the mixture until it's completely warm.

4. Spread a thin layer (1/2 cup) of marinara or enchilada sauce in the bottom of a casserole dish. Place a third of a cup of quinoa mixture in the center of a corn tortilla and roll it up. Place the tortilla, seam down, in the casserole dish. Repeat with all remaining tortillas and then cover them with 3/4 cup of additional sauce. Bake for 25 minutes, and serve.

DESSERT
MEALS

BANANA SOFT SERVE

Makes 2 servings

INGREDIENTS

2 large bananas, peeled and chopped into chunks, then frozen
1/2 teaspoon vanilla

METHOD

Place bananas in a food processor and turn the motor on. Let the processor run until the bananas have gotten increasingly light, fluffy, and smooth. They'll resemble a creamy bowl of soft serve ice cream!

You may need to stop a few times to scrape the bowl down. Be patient, and let the processor do its job — at first it'll seem as though the soft serve isn't coming together, but it will.

Serve with any toppings you like: cacao nibs, dark chocolate, peanut butter, chopped nuts or seeds — the works!

RAW VEGAN BROWNIE BITES

Makes 24-30 balls

INGREDIENTS

2 cups walnuts
2/3 cup cacao nibs
Generous pinch sea salt (to taste)
1/4 cup raw cacao (or regular cocoa) powder
1 1/2 cups pitted dates

METHOD

1. Place the walnuts, cacao nibs, sea salt, and cacao powder in a food processor and process for about 30 seconds, or till everything is pretty well crumbled up.

2. Add the dates and process for another twenty seconds or so. The mixture should be sticking together. If it's not, keep processing till it sticks together easily when you squeeze a little in your hand. If you need to, adding a few more dates will help bind it together.

3. Shape the "dough" into balls that are about 3/4 - 1 inch thick by rolling it in your palms. Store in the fridge for 30 minutes, and then they'll be ready to serve.

Balls will keep, stored in the fridge, for two weeks.

RAW, VEGAN VANILLA MACAROONS

Makes 15 macaroons

INGREDIENTS

1/2 cup raw almonds
1 heaping cup unsweetened, shredded coconut
1/4 cup coconut oil (will be easiest to roll up the macaroons if the oil is solid when you put it in the processor)

3 tablespoons maple syrup
1 teaspoon vanilla extract
Pinch sea salt

METHOD

1. Add almonds to the food processor and process till they're finely ground.

2. Add the remaining ingredients and process again, till everything is well combined.

3. Working quickly (or else the coconut oil will melt) roll the coconut mixture into small (3/4" - 1") balls. Place on a parchment lined platter or baking sheet.

4. Transfer platter to the fridge, and refrigerate for a few hours, till the macaroons are solid. Serve.

Macaroons will keep in the fridge for up to two weeks.

CHOCOMOLE

Serves 2

INGREDIENTS

1 large, ripe Haas avocado, pitted
½ tsp vanilla
4 heaping tablespoons raw cacao powder
3 tbsp maple syrup or agave
1/4 cup water (more as needed)

METHOD

Place all ingredients in a food processor or Vitamix and blend till smooth. Serve.

BLUEBERRY GINGER ICE CREAM

Serves 2

INGREDIENTS

2 frozen bananas
1 heaping cup frozen blueberries
1/2 inch fresh ginger (or 1/2 tsp ginger powder if you're using a food processor)
1/4 cup cashews
2 tsp lemon juice
2-4 tbsp almond or hemp milk

METHOD

Blend all ingredients together in a high speed blender. Start with 2 tbsp of almond milk and use the tamp to try to get the mixture going without adding too much liquid: you want an ice cream, not a smoothie! If you need the extra two tablespoons, use them, but be patient and keep blending with the tamp till a thick consistency is achieved.

22 DAYS NUTRITION

VEGAN CHALLENGE

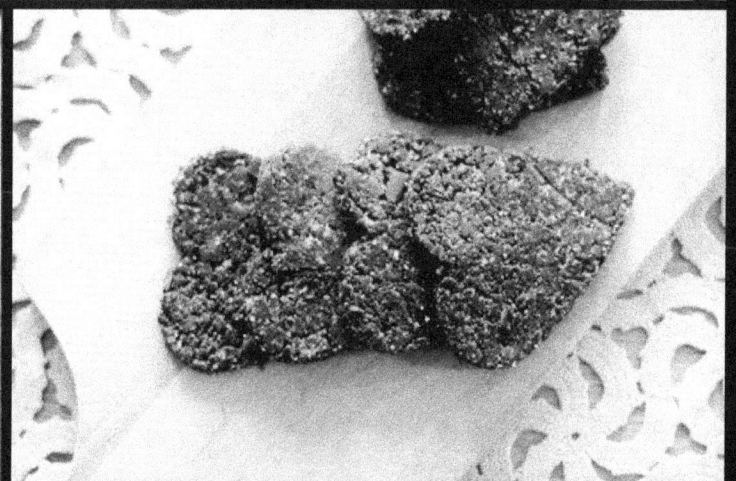

PLANT BASED LIFESTYLE SOLUTIONS

22 DAY MEAL PLAN

Perhaps you are looking to eat healthier and feel more alive. Or reduce your impact on the environment by being more conscious about your food choices. Whatever your reasons, we are here to lead you on the path to exploring a vegan diet.

This guide will set you up with a daily meal plan to experience the benefits of plant-based nutrition for 22 Days. Why 22 Days? It takes 21 days to make or break a habit and by day 22, you've found the way. If you take on the challenge, your body will enjoy a greater variety of vitamins and minerals and your reduced intake of animal products will have a positive effect on the environment.

On the following pages, you'll find 22 Days of vegan meal plans. You'll find that the recipes are easy to prepare, healthy and delicious to boot!

22 DAYS
NUTRITION

VEGAN
MEAL PLAN

22 DAYS
NUTRITION

BREAKFAST: Vanilla chia pudding with 1 cup fresh berries

LUNCH: Crunchy red cabbage and green apple sesame slaw with 1 cup steamed, cubed sweet potato (or 1 small sweet potato, baked)

AFTERNOON SNACK: 1/4 cup hemp hummus with fresh vegetables (carrots, celery, romaine leaves, bell pepper, etc.)

DINNER: Black bean and quinoa salad with quick cumin dressing

DESSERT: Dark chocolate

DAY 2

BREAKFAST: Smoothie with 1 cup almond milk, 1 large frozen banana, 1-2 tablespoons almond butter, 1 serving of 22 Days protein powder, and a heaping cup of leafy greens (spinach, chard, kale, etc.)

LUNCH: 1 brown rice tortilla (Food For Life brand) or two gluten free corn tortillas with 1/4 cup hemp hummus, fresh or roasted red bell pepper, sliced cucumbers, and a handful of greens. Serve with steamed vegetables as desired, or a small side salad.

AFTERNOON SNACK: 22 Days bar

DINNER: Zucchini Pasta with Cherry Tomatoes, Sweet Potato, Basil, and Hemp "Parmesan"

DESSERT: Banana soft serve

DAY 3

BREAKFAST: Quinoa breakfast porridge with 1 cup fresh berries

LUNCH: Large salad with at least three cups of greens, whichever veggies you like, 3 tablespoons pumpkin or hemp seeds, and a dressing of choice (from the dressing options in the recipe index).

AFTERNOON SNACK: 4 tablespoons hemp hummus with fresh vegetables (carrots, celery, romaine leaves, bell pep-per, etc.)

DINNER: Small baked sweet potato (instructions below) with a tablespoon of melted coconut oil, half a cup of organic black beans, and steamed greens as desired (or a fresh side salad)

DESSERT: 2 raw brownie bites

DAY 4

BREAKFAST: 22 Days Peanut Butter & Chocolate Chip Nirvana bar, fresh fruit salad as desired

LUNCH: Golden harvest kale salad with 1/2 cup organic chickpeas

AFTERNOON SNACK: 1 oz. almonds and a few tablespoons raisins

DINNER: Quick white bean and summer vegetable pasta (prepare with quinoa or brown rice pasta)

DESSERT: 2 raw vegan vanilla macaroons

BREAKFAST: Smoothie with 1 cup almond milk, 1 cup frozen blueberries, 1 serving chocolate 22 Days Nutrition protein, 3 tablespoons of hemp seeds, and 1 cup leafy greens of choice

LUNCH: Leftover white bean and summer vegetable pasta or a large green salad with half a cup of beans or lentils, two tablespoons sliced almonds, vegetables of your choosing, and turmeric tahini dressing

AFTERNOON SNACK: Apple with 2 tablespoons almond butter

DINNER: Butternut squash curry served over 1/2 cup cooked quinoa, steamed vegetables as desired

DESSERT: Dark chocolate

DAY 6

BREAKFAST: Banana and almond butter oats (recipe to follow)

LUNCH: Smoky avocado and jicama salad

AFTERNOON SNACK: 1 cup almond milk blended with 22 Days Nutrition protein powder and a few ice cubes

DINNER: Black bean and corn burgers, served with a small salad or steamed vegetables

DESSERT: 2 raw vegan vanilla macaroons

DAY 7

BREAKFAST: Smoothie of 1/2 frozen banana, 1 cup frozen peaches, 2 ice cubes, 3/4 cup almond milk, 1 cup leafy greens, and 1 serving 22 Days Nutrition vanilla protein powder

LUNCH: Leftover black bean and corn burger, small salad

AFTERNOON SNACK: 1/4 cup vegan trail mix of choice (or 2 tbsp raw almonds or cashews and 2 tbsp dried fruit)

DINNER: 1 cup cooked quinoa, brown rice, or millet, served with 1/2 chopped avocado, 1 cup steamed greens, and dressing of choice (from dressing options in recipe index).

DESSERT: 1/2 cup chocomole

DAY 8

BREAKFAST: Gluten free banana pancakes, served with 1 cup fresh berries

LUNCH: Mango, kale, and avocado salad

AFTERNOON SNACK: Apple, banana, melon, berries, or any other fresh fruit of choice

DINNER: Eggplant rollatini with cashew cheese, steamed greens or broccoli as desired

DESSERT: Dark chocolate

BREAKFAST: Apple cinnamon oatmeal

LUNCH: Roasted butternut squash and apple soup, served with a fresh green salad or steamed veggies as desired

AFTERNOON SNACK: 22 Days Nutrition bar

DINNER: Raw zucchini alfredo with basil and cherry tomatoes, served with fresh salad or steamed vegetables as desired

DESSERT: 2 raw vegan brownie bites

DAY 10

BREAKFAST: Smoothie of 1 cup frozen blueberries or mixed berries, 1 cup coconut water, 1/2 small avocado, 1 serving 22 Days Chocolate protein powder, and a dash of cinnamon.

LUNCH: Easy curried yellow lentils with avocado croutons

AFTERNOON SNACK: Fresh vegetable crudites with 1/4 cup hemp hummus

DINNER: Black bean and quinoa salad with quick cumin dressing

DESSERT: 1/2 cup chocomole

DAY 11

BREAKFAST: 1 sliced banana with 1 cup organic puffed rice or millet cereal (I like Arrowhead Mills brand) and 1 cup almond milk

LUNCH: Kale Salad with Apples, Raisins, and Creamy Curry Dressing

AFTERNOON SNACK: 1/4 cup raw trail mix of choice

DINNER: Sweet Potato Lime Burgers, fresh salad or steamed vegetables as desired

DESSERT: 2 raw vanilla macaroons

DAY 12

BREAKFAST: Vanilla chia pudding with 1 cup fresh berries

LUNCH: Red quinoa, almond, and arugula salad with cantaloupe

AFTERNOON SNACK: A couple of raw peanut butter & jelly snack balls

DINNER: Sweet potato and black bean chili with steamed broccoli or greens

DESSERT: 1/2 cup chocomole

DAY 13

BREAKFAST: Smoothie of 1 frozen banana, 1/2 cup frozen mango, 1 heaping cup spinach leaves, 1 cup coconut water, and 1/2 avocado

LUNCH: Bowl of leftover black bean and sweet potato chili with small salad or steamed greens

AFTERNOON SNACK: 22 Days Nutrition bar of choice

DINNER: Cauliflower "rice" with lemon, mint, and pistachios, served over fresh greens

DESSERT: Spicy almond milk hot chocolate

DAY 14

BREAKFAST: Banana and almond butter oats

LUNCH: Carrot avocado bisque with spicy Thai salad

AFTERNOON SNACK: Raw vegetable crudités with sweet potato hummus

DINNER: Brown rice and lentil salad, served with fresh salad or steamed vegetables as desired and dressing of choice

DESSERT: 2 raw vanilla macaroons

DAY 15

BREAKFAST: Strawberry ginger chia pudding

LUNCH: Leftover brown rice and lentil salad, served with a large mixed vegetable salad and dressing of choice from

recipe index.

AFTERNOON SNACK: 2 peanut butter and jelly snack balls

DINNER: Raw "peanut" noodles with steamed vegetables or fresh salad as desired

DESSERT: Dark chocolate

DAY 16

BREAKFAST: Smoothie with 1 cup almond milk, 1 large frozen banana, 1-2 tablespoons almond butter, 1 serving of 22

Days protein powder, and a heaping cup of leafy greens (spinach, chard, kale, etc.)

LUNCH: Mango, kale and avocado salad

AFTERNOON SNACK: Vegetable crudités as desired and 1/4 cup hemp hummus

DINNER: Easy un-fried brown rice and vegetables

DESSERT: 2 raw, vegan brownie bites

DAY 17

BREAKFAST: Banana breakfast wraps

LUNCH: Brown rice tortilla "pizza" and a side salad

AFTERNOON SNACK: 22 Days Nutrition bar

DINNER: Arugula salad with roasted acorn squash, goji berries, and cauliflower

DESSERT: Banana soft serve

DAY 18

BREAKFAST: Apple cinnamon oatmeal

LUNCH: Fennel, avocado, and tomato salad with 1/2 cup chickpeas or white beans

SNACK: 1 cup almond milk blended with 22 Days Protein Powder

DINNER: Roasted vegetable pesto pasta salad

DESSERT: Dark chocolate

DAY 19

BREAKFAST: Gluten free, vegan pumpkin muffins with a tablespoon of almond butter and an apple

LUNCH: Kale Salad with Apples, Raisins, and Creamy Curry Dressing; 1 cup roasted cauliflower and parsnip soup

SNACK: 1/3 cup raw trail mix of choice (or a mix of raw almonds and raisins or goji berries)

DINNER: Raw marinated portobello mushroom "steak" and cauliflower "mashed potatoes," served with steamed greens or broccoli

DESSERT: Blueberry ginger ice cream

DAY 20

BREAKFAST: Smoothie of 1 cup frozen blueberries or mixed berries, 1 cup coconut water, 1/2 small avocado, 1 serving 22Days Chocolate protein powder, and a dash of cinnamon

LUNCH: Easy curried yellow lentils with avocado "croutons," served with a salad and dressing of choice or steamed vegetables as desired

SNACK: Celery sticks served with 2 tablespoons of peanut or almond butter and raisins ("ants on a log" style)

DINNER: Dinner salad of raw greens and vegetables of choosing, 1 cup cooked sweet potato, 1/2 avocado, cubed, 1/2 cup cooked lentils, and a dressing of choice from the recipe index.

DESSERT: 2 raw, vegan brownie bites

DAY 21

BREAKFAST: 1 sliced banana and fresh berries with 1 cup organic puffed rice or millet cereal (I like Arrowhead Mills brand) and 1 cup almond milk

LUNCH: Smoky avocado and jicama salad, 1 small apple if desired

AFTERNOON SNACK: 2 peanut butter and jelly snack balls

DINNER: Quinoa enchiladas

DESSERT: Dark chocolate

BREAKFAST: Smoothie of 1 frozen banana, 1/2 cup frozen mango, 1 heaping cup spinach leaves, 1 cup coconut water, and 1/2 avocado

LUNCH: Leftover quinoa enchilada, side salad with dressing of choice

SNACK: 22 Days Nutrition bar of choice

DINNER: Arugula salad with roasted acorn squash, goji berries, and cauliflower

DESSERT: 2 raw vegan vanilla macaroons